FROM MESS TO MESSAGE

TEN STEPS FOR WRITING YOUR BOOK

KIM ELEY

Eley, Kim. *From Mess to Message: Ten Steps for Writing Your Book*

Copyright © 2023 by Kim Eley

ISBN: 978-1-956092-13-4

KWE Publishing: kwepub.com

CONTENTS

FOREWORD

I'm honored that Kim Eley asked me to write this foreword for her new book. She asked because this book was created from a series of articles Kim wrote for my magazine, *On Purpose Woman*. I said yes because there was so much valuable information in that series that I think it should be shared with a broader audience.

While I've only known Kim for three years and seen her in person maybe six times (you know, the COVID thing), I felt an immediate sisterhood with her. Kim's love of life, her clients, and how she helps them are apparent in all she does. Her humor and her laugh are contagious. She is a kind, generous soul who has found her purpose with the work she brings to the world. Combine these qualities with her writing, publishing, and selling knowledge, and you have a winning combination. She is a perfect person to hold your hand in the highly personal, sometimes scary book creation process.

This book takes you from the "do-I-really-want-to-write-a-book" place to "how to do a book launch." And in between, Kim takes some of the mystery and fear out of writing, publishing, and selling your book.

A lot of people can write a book of "how-tos." What Kim has created is a "how-to with heart." Through her humor, gentleness, straight talk, and vast expertise, she takes you on a journey. This book is much more than an outline of what to do and when to do it —it's a handbook for making decisions, for how to keep moving forward when you get stuck, and for remembering why you're writing your book in the first place. A perfect combination of the practical and the esoteric.

Some of the ways that Kim's book stands out for me:

- She has created a concise, step-by-step guide for the complete book-writing/publishing/selling process.
- She helps you understand why you want to write a book and who will benefit from reading it.
- She uses pregnancy as a perfect metaphor for birthing your book.
- She shares that writing a shitty first draft sure beats not writing at all.
- She gives you ideas on how to end your book.
- She holds your hand through the book launch process, down to what kind of refreshments you might want to serve.

And she shares her brilliance with humor and love.

If Kim Eley can give you this much in a small book, imagine what it could be like working with her in person. So, read this book and see if talking with Kim might be an excellent next step in getting that book out of your head and into the world.

—**Ginny Robertson, Publisher & Founder of** *On Purpose Woman Magazine* **and Founder of the On Purpose Woman Global Community, https://www.opwgc.com**

WHAT ARE YOU WRITING ABOUT? "MISE EN PLACE" FOR YOUR WRITING

There's an amazing concept in French cooking called "mise en place." It literally means "put in place," but it is actually a way to organize all of your ingredients. Chefs recommend having all of your ingredients measured and ready for you to use before you start cooking. We can use the same principles for "mise en place" in our writing by fully understanding what we are writing about, who our audience is, and how we want them to feel once they've read our writing.

You may start by selecting your topic! And now you're ready to roll, right? Yes and no. Yes, hooray, you have selected a topic! But no, while you have a good start, there are a few more decisions for you to make before you start writing. Selecting a topic for your writing is much like choosing a protein before you cook a meal. While you are now focused on the 'meat' of your writing, there are so many ways you can prepare and serve up your writing.

Here's a recipe we can use:

One Juicy Topic, Multiple Ideal Readers, One Consistent Tone

Let's say our *juicy topic* is beekeeping! As a topic, beekeeping offers danger (beestings!), intrigue (how does beekeeping work, anyway?), and also sweet mystery (if I read your writing, can I use what I learn to raise my own honey?). But before you begin writing about beekeeping, you need to ask yourself: *Who are my ideal readers?* Are you reaching out to novice beekeepers who know nothing about the topic? Or are you writing for experienced beekeepers who have mastered the basics and now want to learn advanced techniques? Are you writing for beekeepers who live in a rural setting, or in a big city? Or are you steering away from nonfiction writing altogether and planning to write about a fictitious character who raises bees? (I'm thinking of something similar to **The Beekeeper's Daughter: A Novel**).

Identifying the ideal readers for your book before you begin means your book will cater specifically to their wants and needs. For our beekeeping example, let's say we will write for novice beekeepers in the United States who live in a large city. We'll write a nonfiction book that will include a glossary of beekeeping terms for our newbies (or "newbees!"), so they can learn more and become educated about the topic. The book may also include guidelines for specific U.S. cities, and a reference with websites on beekeeping in cities for additional information. Through our example, we've gotten specific about the topic, which enables us to reach our audience of new U.S. beekeepers living in an urban setting. *Another smart move is getting to know your ideal readers.* Why do the new beekeepers want to take up this new hobby? Are they motivated to save the bees for the environment, are they interested in having fresh honey available, or are they motivated by a combo of both? You can learn more about their motivations by asking people in the demographic for your ideal reader group.

For example, with our novice city-dwelling beekeepers, you could do a Google search for the topics that interest them about beekeeping. Or you could search for Facebook groups on beekeeping and see what their members are writing about. Another source is researching if there is a Meetup group for city beekeepers, and if so, consider attending a meeting. Another approach is to search online for other books about beekeeping. Perhaps there are already other books that exist, but you find they are missing something you feel you can add. Fantastic! Our strategic plan is getting specific. *The next ingredient in our writing recipe is tone.* Do you plan to write a more formal or informal book? Do you feel your readers will appreciate a fun and playful tone? Or do you feel they would prefer a no-nonsense, straightforward approach to reading your book?

Again, consulting your ideal readers is a smart idea. You could do an online search for demographics for your ideal reader. For our example, we could search for the average age of a city-loving wannabe beekeeper. Are they mostly men or women, or is there a pretty even split of both? Are there any additional characteristics they have in common? Knowing the generation (Boomer, Gen X, Millennial, Gen Z, etc.) of your ideal reader will enable you to research what types of books and tones appeal most. Now that you have prepared the ingredients for your writing, I suggest that you keep a list of your ideal readers' characteristics, your intention, and your tone next to you as you write. This list is your organized mise en place, and having it available means you are ready to write!

To continue our example, once I was ready to start writing about novice beekeepers raising hives in U.S. cities, I would keep a list similar to this one handy as a reminder:

- **Ideal reader is a novice beekeeper who lives in a large city that allows its residents to raise bees at their downtown residences.**
- **They are about 45-55 years old, a Gen Xer, which means they love stories that tug at their heartstrings, such as saving the bees who have been threatened by a condition called colony collapse.**
- **They also like a direct and clear approach, so nonfiction writing with direct tips for beekeeping would appeal.**

I hope this example gives you some insight into how to prepare for your writing. With much of the thought work done upfront with the mise en place technique, it becomes easier to stick to your topic, tone, and approach. Your ideal readers will be receptive to reading your message! I encourage you to start cooking up your incredible writing today!

INVESTING IN A BOOK PAYS OFF: HOW MUCH TIME AND MONEY SHOULD YOU SPEND ON SELF-PUBLISHING?

Now more than ever, writing and self-publishing your book is one of the most powerful ways to grow your business and make money. But first, I want to share with you a secret I tell all of my clients.

The Real Money in Books

This secret is so significant that I call it having "The Talk." No, it is not about the birds and bees! What I share with my clients is that most authors don't make significant amounts of money from their online book sales! Unless you are a big-name author, the market is so saturated that book sales are often low.

However, writing and self-publishing books can indeed make you money! What's the scoop? Entrepreneurs make money when they use their books as their BEST MARKETING TOOL EVER!

The money to be made from self-publishing books comes from establishing yourself as an expert, attracting and getting hired by clients, raising your visibility, getting media coverage, and gifting copies to event planners and employers. I call books your business card on steroids. If there are so many advantages to writing and self-publishing books, what's stopping many entrepreneurs from writing theirs? The answer is the investment of time, money, and skills.

Taking the Time to Write and Publish

How long it takes to write a book depends on the writer and their abilities. The most successful writers, meaning the ones who start and actually finish their books, create a plan. By establishing a writing habit, they complete their writing by a certain date to meet their planned schedule.

After a writer completes their book draft, how long does it take to self-publish? On average, it takes about seven months. A number of steps, including editing, formatting, proofreading, and ordering printed proofs, must be completed prior to publishing. Additional subtasks involved in a book project include ordering International Standard Book Numbers (ISBNs), choosing keywords and the correct genres, and registering the book with the Library of Congress (LOC), to name a few.

Which Writing/Publishing Role Suits You?

I've run into many people who have written and self-published books and were completely frustrated by the process! Whether you love or hate to write, or are intimidated by the self-publishing process, you can still get your words out with your amazing book. Let's look at three approaches to writing and self-publishing. I have named each approach as a role, provided a description, and added my tips for investing in a self-published book based on these characteristics.

A *DIY Diva* has the time and the know-how to write and publish her own book. Savvy with tech skills, she has the confidence to tackle the aspects of self-publishing.

- Project management—She can plan all of the milestones and deadlines for writing her book.

- Accountability—She has established a writing habit, and she sticks to it.
- Research—She has read books about self-publishing and makes the time to do research.
- Thriftiness—She has amazing friends and colleagues who are willing to pitch in with help, which may include (good) editing and book cover design.

Recommendation: The *DIY Diva* has the confidence, time, and know-how to write and self-publish her book with minimal monetary investment ($0-500). She would rather do the legwork herself when it comes to the administrative parts of publishing (ISBNs, copyrighting, etc.) than pay for someone else to do the work. Depending on her technical skill level, her time investment may be heavier than seven months.

A *Time-Crunched Task Master* has the know-how and discipline to write her draft, but she employs others when it's time to self-publish. Balancing her time and monetary resources, she would rather hire a publishing consultant to do the work needed for publishing.

- Project management—She can plan all of the milestones and deadlines for writing her book.
- Accountability—She's established a writing habit, and she sticks to it.
- Practicality—She knows it is worth it to pay an editor, a publishing consultant, and whomever she needs to collaborate on her book once she's written the draft. She may be able to accomplish some tasks herself but engages others for ones outside her "zone of genius."

Recommendation: She can write and self-publish her book with modest monetary investment ($500-2500). How much she spends will depend on the contractors she hires. She may need to be hands-on. If she uses multiple contractors (from companies like Fiverr or Upwork, for example) to assist her.

To a *Dynamic Delegator*, hiring a writing coach to help her stay accountable is the smartest decision. She may consider employing a ghostwriter. She prefers to work with a publisher or publishing consultant who will take care of all of the tasks, milestones, and deadlines for writing and publishing her book. She knows the money she invests will pay off in the client acquisitions she will obtain from her book and time spent in developing other projects.

- Project delegation—She saves herself valuable time and spares herself from frustration by collaborating with and delegating the accountability for writing her draft to her writing coach or ghostwriter.
- Practicality—She knows it is worth it to pay an editor and to work with a publishing consultant or publisher to complete her book and publish it once she's written her draft.

Recommendation: Saving herself aggravation and time is the driver for the Dynamic Delegator. Her monetary investment will depend on the writing coach or ghostwriter she hires ($900-15,000). Working with a publishing consultant or publisher means she can focus on the message of her book and let the experts tackle the publishing tasks.

Of course, these are general guidelines, but they illustrate considerations about your investment of time and money and your skill level. My hope is that you will write your business card on steroids and make your book your BEST MARKETING TOOL EVER!

THE SPECIAL INGREDIENT FOR WRITING SUCCESS

I was shocked to learn that 97% of people who start to write a book never finish it. When you do the math, that means out of 1000 people who start, only 30 complete their books. *That's heartbreaking.* As a writing coach, I know the special ingredient you need to start and keep writing. Surprisingly, I rarely hear other writers and coaches discussing this topic in relation to writing. But with it, writers can develop a solid foundation for their writing projects. What do you think it might be?

- A strong and engaging first sentence?
- A well-developed outline?
- A strategic plan identifying your ideal reader?

If you answered yes to one or more of these options, you are partially correct. All of these options are important, and we will discuss each of them later. However, they come after the first, somewhat surprising ingredient. And that ingredient is *confidence.*

Why Haven't You Started?

Do you remember a time when you had to write something, and it made you feel uncomfortable? Maybe it was a school essay or a paper for work. Think about the reasons you felt uncomfortable.

- Were you thinking about the importance of your message?
- Were you caught up with thinking how much you felt like you wanted your words to make an impact?
- Did you think about the stakes involved once you shared your writing with another person?
- While you were writing, did you think about that teacher, boss, or coworker who would read your words later and judge them?

Writing is communication. When someone reads what you've written, they either get it, or they don't. The effectiveness of what you have written is immediate once it is read. In the world of gymnastics, have you heard the term "stick the landing"? For gymnasts, "sticking" the landing means successfully completing a movement or pose and landing without moving your feet at the end.

As writers, we can "stick" the landing in our writing, meaning successfully conveying our message in as few words as needed to be understood. It is understandable that we would experience hesitation when we are writing. Our uncertainty lies in the draft when we want to express our thoughts to a reader, but we are not sure how our words will land. How we express ourselves are representations of us, who we are, and who we want to be. We may long to be seen as a gymnast of words, someone whose command and craft of language dazzles our audience. Building up this sort of pressure on ourselves can cause a lot of needless anxiety, however.

Why Do You Want to Write?

I truly believe each of us is here on earth because we have a powerful message to share. We can express our message through our work, through our love and care for others, and through our unique gifts. And of course, we can share our message through our writing too. When you are feeling unsure about your writing, think about why you want to write. Imagine another person reading your words.

- What impact do you want them to have?
- Do you want their heart to leap for joy?
- Do you want them to stop partway through and exclaim, "Aha! I've got it now! It all makes sense!"
- Do you want them to be so moved by the power of your words that they cease to live their lives the way they did and feel transformed?

You don't have to imagine. You can make these results happen.

You Are a Writer, and Your Words Have Power

How often have you started writing something, only to tell yourself, "I'm not a writer!"? It's not pretty, but we do tend to have some crappy voices in our heads telling us garbage. We will think, "Well, I'm not very good at this." Or, "I just don't know how to say this." Without empowering your voice, you risk building your writing on anxiety, fear, and a wicked case of perfectionism. Own your voice. First, I want you to say out loud, "I am a writer, and my words have power." What you say out loud is believed by your subconscious mind. So even if you might feel silly doing this, I want you to say these words out loud. When those lousy voices come back, bringing doubts, say the words out loud again: "I am a writer, and my words have power."

Build Onto Your Confidence Foundation

Now you are standing tall in your own words. You own your voice! Now what? Your confident writer self can take the lead by using the tools in your writing tool belt. We touched on a few of these earlier:

- A strong and engaging first sentence
- A well-developed outline
- A strategic plan identifying your ideal reader

You've often heard that first impressions count when you meet someone for the first time. Think of your first sentence in your writing as your introduction to your reader. Here are some options for making the introduction:

- Shake long-held beliefs by presenting them with a fact or idea they have never known.
- Pull at their heartstrings by showing them something about which they should care deeply.
- Challenge your readers by expressing the unfairness of a practice or situation.

I'll let you in on a secret. All of these tools for generating a memorable first sentence involve generating emotion. Your confidence as a writer is in knowing that you can generate a feeling or passion from your reader. Each time you write, remember that you have the power to stoke that fire in someone whom you may never meet face to face. It is your words that resonate with your reader. You own this power. After your first engaging sentence, you will have your readers' attention. Next, it is time to "stick the landing" by ensuring your entire message is clear. You make sure your message is clear by using a well-developed outline. Like a roadmap, a good outline shows you as the writer where to go with your writing essay. You've got the confidence at this point to take the reader where you want to go. With your outline, you will ensure you and your reader visit each point you want to make. That will be the evidence you need to "stick the landing" with your reader, ensuring their understanding.

Finally, you want a strategic plan to identify your ideal reader. Using different magazines as examples, I believe we can all agree that the ideal reader for *Popular Mechanics* may be quite different from the ideal reader of *People* magazine. Are you writing for gearheads or celebrity followers? Know who your reader is, and you'll find a way to talk with them.

Why Are You Waiting? Jump In and Write!

Once you own that you are a writer, then you will gain the confidence to continue writing no matter what. On days when you have something you've committed to writing, say a standing blog post, you may hear those old voices that made you feel uncomfortable. Remember these steps:

- Say out loud, "I am a writer, and my words have power!"
- Hook them right from the start with a captivating first sentence.
- Map out all of the ideas you will explore in your outline.
- Know your reader and write in a way she will enjoy and respond to.

You have an incredible message to share! Get started, and write!

WHAT TO EXPECT WHEN YOU'RE PUBLISHING A BOOK

My phone pinged as I received a text: *"I'm pregnant!"*

What? I thought.

My girlfriend stunned me with her words. *Wow, she's not in a relationship. Her two daughters are adults. And she's in her fifties, like me...*

As I sat with my jaw hanging down in shock, she quickly sent a follow-up text:

"With a book idea!"

OHHHHHHHHHHHHHHHH! I set my phone down and laughed out loud. Afterward, I couldn't stop thinking about the similarities between birthing a child and publishing. My mind began racing as I created a mental list.

With books:

- You become "pregnant" with an idea.
- You begin developing the story, and it grows until it is fully formed.

- It often takes months (and sometimes years) to develop.
- Often, you are unsure what to anticipate.
- You give "birth" when you release your manuscript.
- You are a proud "parent" once your book is released.

Many prospective authors contact me and say, "I don't know where to get started!" Their statement makes me think about the famous book about pregnancy, *What to Expect When You're Expecting*. While I am not a mother, I have been a "book doula" for a number of books, working with writers from idea to book launch and enabling them to "birth" their books. From my experience as a writing coach and publisher, here is what I can share so you know what to expect when you're publishing a book.

You have an idea – now what?

As my friend described, you become "pregnant" with an idea for a book. Once you know your idea, frequently, it dominates your thoughts until you feel compelled to take action. It's time to write!

The first step I suggest you think about is what you will do with your book idea if you publish it.

Is it a passion project, or will you use your book to promote your business?

Will you only share your printed book with friends and family members, or will you publish it to booksellers and online retailers for sale?

The decisions you make will determine the scope of your book project and how to proceed.

Picking Out a Name

I'm surprised how often writers already have a title in mind for their book without having written a word. "I haven't started," they share with me, "but I've got the title picked out."

I often advise my clients to choose a title and subtitle using a test I call the **"Huh?/Oh!"** approach. Your title should be something sticky, something memorable that intrigues your reader, making them say, "Huh?" Great titles have lasting power, and you want yours to be memorable.

After choosing a great title, select a subtitle to explain what your book title is about. Your subtitle gives more clues about your content. Your subtitle should make your reader exclaim, "Oh!" as they gain a better understanding of your title or your idea for your book.

I'll share an example of a book that I believe brilliantly passes the "Huh?/Oh!" test for its title and subtitle. Elizabeth Gilbert famously wrote the book, *Eat, Pray, Love*. The title is intriguing, and the first time you encountered it, it likely made you say, "Huh?" It's not immediately apparent what eating, praying, and loving have to do with one another. The subtitle she chose, *One Woman's Search for Everything Across Italy, India and Indonesia,* illuminates the reader on what the book is about. The reader knows to expect a quest for knowledge and an international adventure. While the title is catchy, the subtitle offers more insights.

I have often heard when someone chooses a name for a child, they should stand on their back porch and yell the name to see if they like the sound of it. This is suggested because a parent may often shout their child's name while calling them. While you will not need to scream your book's name to call it into your house, as an author, you will be sharing your book's name frequently. Be sure it is a name you like.

Another identifier for your book is an ISBN, or International Standard Book Number. You need to assign an ISBN to your book in order to sell it. You can think of it as the Social Security Number for your book.

If you want to publish your book with online retailers, you must obtain an ISBN. If you work with a publisher, they generally provide you with your ISBNs. If you are self-publishing, you have two choices. You can either choose an ISBN through the publishing company you use to self-publish, or you can purchase your own ISBN through Bowker. Bowker is the sole provider of ISBNs for the United States and other parts of the world. You can buy ISBN numbers at their website, www.bowker.com. When you purchase your own ISBNs, you own the rights to your book, which is preferable.

Choose a Team

When you are expecting a book, it's a smart idea to choose a team to help you. While you can write and publish your book alone, hiring others can make your book publishing journey easier, more efficient, and less painful. Here are some people you may consider adding to your team:

- *Writing Coach*

A writing coach enables you to organize your ideas for your book and choose a direction to take. They will act as an accountability partner, helping you stick to your publishing goals and deadlines. As a skilled writer themselves, your writing coach can answer your writing questions.

- *Editor*

A good editor is worth their weight in gold! When you hire an editor, they review your manuscript for content. They will offer comments and suggestions to improve your writing. You want a great editor to collaborate with you to craft your story in a way that is compelling, clearly written, and free from errors.

- *Virtual Author's Assistant*

When you hire a virtual author's assistant, you count on them to tackle your social media, publicity, marketing for your book, and other administrative tasks. This is a huge help with all of the many aspects involved in publishing. Depending on your needs, you can hire a virtual assistant for several hours a month or week.

- *Publisher*

A publisher is a project manager for your book. They set up the timelines for every step of the process and act as the central point of contact for the editors, graphic designers, printers, and others on your team. There are three types of book publishers: traditional, self-publishers, and hybrid publishers.

- *Book Marketer*

Book marketers are crucial to getting the word out about your book. They enable you to identify your ideal reader, discover the best ways to reach your readers, and analyze the effectiveness of your results. They do the work of narrowing your focus so you are selling your book to the readers with whom your message will most resonate.

- *Book Publicist*

The goal of a book publicist is to drum up interest and excitement surrounding your book. They create awareness through media interviews, featured stories, book reviews, and articles.

Anticipate months of work

While you may feel on fire about your book idea, know that it will take time to write, edit, format, and publish your book. Getting the idea can be fun and relatively quick (like conception) versus the process of publishing the book (which can take months, like carrying a child).

There are many parts to the publishing process:

- Creating an outline
- Crafting a strategic plan
- Writing your shitty first draft
- Reviewing and editing
- Formatting
- Creating a cover

- Marketing
- Public relations
- Book launch

Anticipate that it will take time to write your book. If you are self-publishing, you'll need to schedule time for tasks such as choosing keywords, selecting the right genres, ordering a printed proof, and other tasks that may not be immediately visible on your to-do list.

Ultimately, all the pain will be worth it

Yes, there is labor involved in writing a book. Trust me when I say it is all worth it. When you hold your printed book in your hands for the first time, it is an amazing feeling.

WRITE IT SHITTY! THE FIRST DRAFT BELONGS TO THE UNIVERSE

ARRGGGGGHHHH! With a giant heave ho, I angrily threw away a huge bag of perfectly good, expensive knitting needles and yarn into the dumpster. I tried to teach myself the craft by using a book and it was awful. With tears of frustration, I described the incident to my friend at work, adding that "knitting is an evil activity and no one should do it." Once she talked me off the emotional ledge, she offered to teach me how to knit.

Thus started a weekly session we called "Stitch and Bitch." Every Wednesday, we'd meet at lunchtime in one of the conference rooms at work. My patient friend taught me (and later other curious co-workers) the art of knitting. Feeling more confident with my friend's over-the-shoulder instructions, I started making a hat. And at the end, when I finished it…well, it sucked.

We called it the "ugly dog-walking hat." Lord help any dog walker who might wear that holey mess! There were gaps you could stick your thumb through. I became emotional and was headed to the nearest trashcan with it when my friend held up her hand and yelled, "STOP!"

Then, she proceeded to explain that the first attempt at anything creative is an offering to the Universe.

Puzzled, I sat down and listened. "Everyone has to get the creativity out of their system for their first project," she explained kindly. "Your first attempt at knitting is going to be awful. Offer it as a gift to the Universe. It shows the Universe that you were serious and meant it when you tried to create this hat. Offer this hat to the Universe, and start again."

Immediately, my shoulders loosened, and I started breathing normally again. And later, as I relayed this story, another friend wisely pointed out, "Well, did you really expect to be perfect at knitting the first time you tried it?" Once she put it that way, I had to laugh at myself for getting upset.

I love knitting now, and I also love writing. But writing is like starting a new project every time you put pen to paper. We are not going to magically unfurl a beautiful string of words, pearls of wisdom effortlessly flowing from our brains through our hands and onto the page. Nope.

Instead, we always write a shitty first draft.

I wish I could claim this clever phrase, but I borrowed it from the amazing author, Anne Lamott. It's from her book, *Bird by Bird: Some Instructions on Writing and Life.* In this marvelous book, which I encourage every writer to read, she includes a chapter called "Shitty First Drafts." She explains:

People tend to look at successful writers, writers who are getting their books published and maybe even doing well financially, and think that they sit down at their desks every morning feeling like a million dollars, feeling great about who they are and how much talent they have and what a great story they have to tell; that they take in a few deep breaths, push back their sleeves, roll their necks a few times to get all the cricks out, and dive in, typing fully formed passages as fast as a court reporter. But this is just the fantasy of the uninitiated.

I have to confess that I spit out my coffee the first time I read this. I was one of those uninitiated who assumed that there were people in this world who were born with a muse. Yes, a muse, one of the mythical Greek goddesses who rule over the arts and whisper best-sellers into Stephen King's ears. I had always thought, *Gosh, how lucky that some people can just sit down and bang out a masterpiece.*

There's no luck to it at all, actually. This passage by Anne Lamott reminds me that so many things in life are disguised to look perfect. For example, social media is filled with smiling people in gorgeous clothes who look like their day is just easy-breezy-lemon-squeezy, right? But you know darn well that in reality, everyone has bad hair days, pants that split, and children with behavior so horrific that they could easily be mistaken for Satan's spawn. But the thing is – no one is going to take or post those types of pictures! These posters didn't luck out and only take perfect photos. They chose to only post the edited, pretty photos.

Next time you are ready to write, I want you to picture your favorite writer. Instead of a dreamy fantasy of them with wonderful words pouring out like honey, imagine them sitting at laptop, having the same struggle you do. They sit in front of their piece of paper or blank Word document file and feel a little shudder. *OMG, I so want this to be perfect,* they think. And then they write their shitty first draft.

This is the secret. The real magic in writing does not come during the first draft. The first draft is like a lump of misshapen Play-Doh. You may look at it the way I gazed at the ugly dog walking hat, like, "What? I made all this effort just to create this crappola?"

I want you to look again. Anne Lamott shared that all writers create shitty first drafts.

All good writers write them. This is how they end up with good second drafts and terrific third drafts.

There is no muse who somehow mixed up your address in their GPS and skipped your house. It's up to you to keep working and sweating it out. I challenge you to write that initial gift to the Universe, to show you mean business when you write, and put it out there in a shitty way for the first draft. Once you're done, and you perform the real magic of editing, you'll be ready to share your beautiful, Instagram-worthy pretty seventh draft.

IF YOU DON'T KNOW WHERE YOU'RE GOING, YOU WON'T GET THERE

Waiting for creative magic to happen when you write? Have you ever heard someone say they are waiting for the creative muse to visit?

While researching writing accountability groups, I found a marvelous book called *WAG Your Work* by Kimberly A. Skarupski, Ph.D., MPH. In her book, Dr. Skarupski includes this delightful description of this expectation many writers have:

The muse myth is the idea that there's some tiny, sparkly writing fairy princess who lives up in the heavens. When she hears us emphatically state, 'Now, I shall write!' she flies her bedazzled pixie wings over and showers us with writing fairy dust, trilling, 'Yes, yes, write, sweetheart! Write like the wind!' Then all of a sudden, there's a mystical, swirling vortex of brain cotton candy and we're like, 'Whoa! It's happening! I have the power!' The words start spilling out of us like silk and liquid gold, and our brains and fingers are en fuego! We are brilliant, and no more eloquent words have ever been banged upon a keyboard!

If you're currently thinking, *I have GOT to get my hot little hands on this muse!* I have some sour news. She doesn't exist. Dr. Skarupski explains:

There's nothing magical about writing, but we tend to think there's something special about it.

While magic is not involved in writing, we do have two powerful tools that can enable us to focus our writing, identify who we want to reach, and create a roadmap for how to get there.

These tools are your outline and your strategic plan.

When you read about creating an outline, are you stricken with heart palpitations and middle school flashbacks? That's normal because many of us learned how to create an outline when we were around twelve or thirteen. And some of us have terrible memories of learning to outline.

If you are one of these people, I'd like to reintroduce you to the outline. It could just become your new writing BFF.

Outlines are fantastic because they are the Marie Kondo for your ideas. If you aren't familiar, Marie Kondo is a Japanese consultant who wrote a book, *The Life-Changing Magic of Tidying Up*, about organizing one's home. In her book, she suggests getting rid of anything that doesn't "spark joy." By following her suggestions, even useful household items can be chucked aside or given away if you do not look forward to seeing them every day.

I love this principle, and I believe we can adopt it for our writing. While we as writers want to engage our readers, we cannot do this unless we are engaged in our own writing. In other words, if your writing doesn't bring joy to you, it will not bring joy to your readers.

Think of your outline, which is essentially a tool for organizing ideas, as a large storage container. And imagine you have another storage container right next to your Outline box for the ideas you get rid of. We'll call this box the Parking Lot because we are parking ideas here.

As you sort through the mental clutter in your brain related to your book, imagine you have these two containers in front of you, Outline and Parking Lot. You can even grab a sheet of paper, draw a line down the middle, and put "Outline" and "Parking Lot" as the titles for each column.

As you think about your book topic, which ideas resonate with you? Think about each topic, and then see how your gut reacts to each topic. For an idea to resonate or "spark joy," it should make you feel excited. Your brain should start whirring away, thinking, *Hey, if I write about this topic, then I can write about this, and that, and...* This idea is Outline-worthy, so write it in that column on your piece of paper.

On the flip side, if you think of any ideas and it makes you feel "meh," that idea is not sparking joy, sister. Write down that puppy in your Parking Lot container. Keep them for a while, but if they never spark joy, you know what to do.

Once you've completed your list, stop and look at what you've written. The outline ideas you've captured are a wonderful list of great thoughts. Now you can start arranging these ideas into a logical order. I like writing each idea onto an index card, enabling you to move around the ideas in front of you and play with different orders. You can have major topics, subtopics, and supporting details on these cards.

Once you arrange your cards in a logical order, boom! You have your outline.

You might think you are ready to write once you have your outline. Not so fast! I encourage you to take an extra step. Yes, your outline allows you to write from topic to topic in an organized way. But your outline doesn't answer crucial questions about *why* you are writing.

Think of your book writing project as a road trip. Let's pretend we are driving to Key West! Your outline is like your GPS to get you where you are going, down Route 1 to the Florida Keys. But while your GPS can tell you *where* you are going, it doesn't tell you *why* you are going, or what you plan to *do* in Key West when you get there. Are you planning a fun girls' trip to Key West, or going on a family vacation with your kiddos? I think we can agree that planning a girls' trip (margaritas and late nights) is usually much different than creating a fun family experience (water sports and kid-friendly activities).

To supplement your outline, once you select your book topic, begin creating a strategic plan. Your strategic plan includes identifying your book's:

- Intention
- Message
- Ideal Reader

Your intention is what you want to do with your book. Do you want your readers to take action after they read it? Do you want to elicit a specific feeling or thought? That's your intention.

Your message is what you want to say. If you write about women leaders, that's a great topic. But you want to make your message specific. Are you writing about why women are great leaders or capturing stories about women leaders in history? Same topic, different message.

Finally, you want to know who you believe will read your book. If you write a book about vineyards, are you writing for people unfamiliar with drinking wine, or are you writing a book for wine aficionados? Considering who your ideal reader will be helps you make a book that will really appeal to them.

When you become focused on your intention, message, and ideal reader, you capture your *why* for your book. It distills your purpose for writing, and enables you to keep that in mind during your writing process. Immediately you become focused, goal-oriented. You know who will be reading your book, what feeling or thinking state you want them to have, and what your real message is.

Along with their book outline, the Strategic Plan is what I use to guide my amazing clients to their book destination. Know where you are going before you write, and you'll be amazed at the places you'll go!

STOP! ENDING YOUR BOOK IS HARD TO DO

So we beat on, boats against the current, borne back ceaselessly into the past.

If you recognize this sentence, you may be having a flashback from your high school English class. Haunting and memorable, this last sentence from *The Great Gatsby* by F. Scott Fitzgerald is arguably one of the best endings of an American novel.

As writers, we often focus on crafting a killer first sentence. We want to hook our readers, engaging them right from the start. By contrast, I find that we don't discuss how to end your book as much as how to start it. Yet it's an important topic that deserves some focus. Authors have a responsibility to disembark their readers in a similar way as they embarked. You want to have an ending that grips your readers' imagination and makes them continue to think about and discuss your book.

With that in mind, let's explore how to end your amazing book.

What should my book's word count be? Let's look at suggested book lengths by genre:

General Fiction

- **Flash Fiction:** 300–1500 words
- **Short Story:** 1500–30,000 words
- **Novellas:** 30,000–50,000 words
- **Novels:** 50,000–110,000 words

Fiction Genres

- **Mainstream Romance:** 70,000–100,000 words
- **Subgenre Romance:** 40,000–100,000 words
- **Science Fiction / Fantasy:** 90,000–120,000 (and sometimes 150,000) words
- **Historical Fiction:** 80,000–100,000
- **Thrillers / Horror / Mysteries / Crime:** 70,000–90,000 words
- **Young Adult:** 50,000–80,000

Children's Books

- **Picture Books:** 300–800 words
- **Early Readers:** 200–3500 words
- **Chapter Books:** 4000–10,000 words
- **Middle Grade:** 25,000–40,000 words

Nonfiction

- **Standard Nonfiction** (Business, Political Science, Psychology, History, etc.): 70,000–80,000 words
- **Memoir:** 80,000–100,000 words
- **Biography:** 80,000–200,000 words
- **How-to / Self-Help:** 40,000–50,000 words

WHILE THESE ARE the recommended lengths, recognize that they are just guidelines, not literary laws. It is more important to write in a clear, concise way than it is to add words to meet a quota. Never write additional verbiage solely to meet a word-length guideline. Shoveling in "filler" will bog down the writing you have so carefully crafted.

Consult Your Strategic Plan

When I work with awesome author clients, we start creating their books by using a strategic plan. I discussed this plan in the previous chapter, "If You Don't Know Where You're Going, You Won't Get There." To recap, when we start a book together, my clients and I identify three main components:

- Intention
- Message
- Ideal reader

Throughout the writing process, we use their strategic plan to double-check we are on track. As we write and review each chapter, we will ask ourselves, "Is this chapter focusing on the book's intention? Will my ideal reader respond to this? Will this passage resonate with them, or will the readers be confused? Is this passage supporting my message?"

Once we reach the end of their book, my clients and I do one last review of their strategic plan. We read their chapters from start to finish and see if their message is consistent and achieves the goal of their plan. If any part of the book falls short, we review that passage and rewrite it until we are satisfied.

Tie Up All Loose Ends

In the beginning of a nonfiction book, most authors describe the points they plan to make. In fiction books, there are often lots of characters who are introduced, described, and interact with each other. No matter whether you write nonfiction or fiction, you want to tie up all of the loose ends.

After we review their strategic plan, my awesome author clients and I look at their outline. Did we address each point they want to discuss in their nonfiction book? In their novel, are the characters consistent? Are all of the plotlines resolved? What works and what doesn't?

This is an important part of your editing process. If you keep in mind the points you want to make, or the storylines you have crafted, and fail to tie up the loose ends, it can frustrate your reader. There is one important exception to this, however, which is creating a cliffhanger.

Cliffhangers

Cliffhangers are book endings in fiction that end at a particular point where the story is not completely resolved. A great cliffhanger leaves your reader wanting more in a great way. Often used in trilogies or book series, cliffhangers stop the action at the end of one book so it can be continued in the next book in the series.

In fiction, it is a good idea to tell the rest of the story from the previous book that ended on a cliffhanger. Your reader will want to know what happened when they start reading the next book in your series. If you don't address the cliffhanger in your next book, your readers will be upset. No one likes remaining in suspense for too long!

Share with Beta Readers

If you want to get feedback on your book and its ending, consider asking for people to be beta readers for you. Similar to a movie screening with a test audience, having beta readers review your book will give you valuable feedback prior to publishing.

Beta readers will share what works and what doesn't in your book. They may ask questions about your content or characters you had not thought about. When you receive their comments, you have the opportunity to update your manuscript accordingly. It is important to choose beta readers who enjoy or have expertise in the genre in which you are writing.

Always accept beta readers' feedback with gratitude as they are helping you craft your best book. However, if you disagree with their ideas, keep in mind that we all have our own opinions about what works and what doesn't. Consider their reviews and thoughtfully decide whether to act on their suggestions. If you have several readers who express confusion about your ending, that's a good sign you may want to change it, for instance.

You can ask trusted friends and family to be beta readers. In addition, there are beta readers who advertise their skills for hire on online sites. Be sure to vet someone carefully before sharing your manuscript with them. Also, I recommend asking beta readers to sign a non-disclosure agreement if you do not know them well.

The End

When you are sharing your incredible book message, think about the way you want your readers to react. Do you want them to wail from sorrow, to feel light as a feather and inspired, or to drool from the anticipation of a great cliffhanger? Keeping your reader in mind as you craft your ending will make a huge impression, similar to boats on the current, borne back ceaselessly into your readers' souls.

LAUNCHING YOUR AMAZING BOOK! CELEBRATE YOUR SUCCESS

In October 2019, my client, Brian Muka, and I launched his first book, *Your Secret Superpower: Tame Fear to Thrive.* As a life coach and "fear sherpa," he highlighted his background as a military paratrooper in the pages of his book. And he wanted to use it as the theme of this event.

Nervously, the guests walked into the airplane hangar, not sure what to expect. As Brian and I greeted them, the air was charged with anticipation. This, you see, was going to be a unique book launch.

WHAT IS A BOOK LAUNCH? There are a couple of definitions I want to share with you.

When you are publishing a book, the first definition of a book launch is your launch date, which is your date of publication. This is the day when your book is officially made available. If you are self-publishing, you get to decide when your book gets published. If you work with a traditional publisher, they often choose the date for you. This is helpful for doing marketing and other book-related promotions. Having your launch date allows you to let people know when to expect your book.

The second definition of a book launch is a book launch party. A book launch party combines a book signing and a celebration of your book's debut. Sometimes your book launch event is held on the exact same day as your publication launch, but it isn't a requirement.

Let's going to focus on the second definition, the book launch party.

I like to think of your book launch party as a well-deserved celebration for family and friends who have patiently put up with you as you worked on your book! They have cheered you on and this is your chance to express your gratitude. And it is a wonderful opportunity for you to celebrate your incredible accomplishment of finishing your book. Did you realize that 81% of people polled in 2002 said they wanted to write a book? Yet 90% of writers fail at achieving this dream. Once you know these statistics, you realize you really have a reason to celebrate when you publish your book.

As a writing coach and publisher, I love celebrating with my awesome authors. We schedule the book launch parties to last for about two hours. Often, we met in person, although you can also have a great virtual book launch, too. Authors may invite as many or few people as they'd like. I like to choose a location that coordinates well with the theme or intention of the author's book. Here are some examples from my clientele:

- For a leadership coach, we launched her book at a yoga studio. The relaxed energy matched her vibe.
- For a Christian nonfiction writer, we held a book launch at a coffee shop. The atmosphere was warm and welcoming and encouraged conversation, which matched her book style.
- For an executive who wrote her memoir and weaved in stories about wine, we partnered with a local vineyard. Her book launch was part of a wine-tasting event.

Since this is a party, you can certainly have food and beverages.

You can include whatever feels most festive and appropriate. For virtual book launches, we incorporate fun party-style games for the attendees.

I usually recommend an agenda for your book launch party so it has a bit of structure. That way, your guests know what to expect. I suggest that authors spend the first half hour of their two-hour event meeting and greeting guests as they come in. It's fun to say hello to everybody and make them feel welcome. About thirty minutes into the party, I recommend having a book reading. Gather all of your guests around and say something like, "Hey, everybody, so glad you're here. I'm going to read an excerpt from my book." Arrange chairs and locate a central place where you can stand and read from your book. After the book reading, people will start milling around and talking again.

At in-person events, we always set up a table where authors can sell copies of their books. I generally recommend that you have a couple of chairs behind your table, a sign displaying how much each book costs, Sharpie pens for signing your books, and a way to take in money. I recommend that authors obtain a Square or other devices for charging credit cards. It's also a good idea to bring a money box in which you have brought small denominations of bills for change. Another good tip is to invite another person to join you. It's great to create a flow at the book signing table so people line up, purchase a copy of your book, and your helper can accept payment while you are signing your books.

About an hour and a half into the event, I like to announce a second book reading where you as the author read a different section from your book. Right after you complete your second reading, you can thank everyone and acknowledge the people who helped you get to the finish line with your book. You may even want to invite others to come up and speak.

IN 2019, after Brian and I chose to launch his book about fear at the small Dinwiddie County Airport, headquarters of the Virginia

Skydiving Center, the rest of the logistics were easy. A sofa, some chairs, and a podium were our requests for his event. We wanted a place for everyone to sit and a spot for the speakers to talk. He invited his parents who attended from New Jersey.

The hangar was the perfect setting for Brian to discuss how he wrote his story and to talk about his mission: empowering others to embrace fear and use it as a superpower. Brian read several passages from his book. After Brian read, several of his family members, friends, and I spoke. Then it was time for our main event.

Half of our attendees suited up and prepped. The other half of the group waved us farewell as we boarded a small plane. And then, up and up we went! And Brian, his friends, and I jumped out of an airplane! Yes, we held a skydiving book launch for Brian's amazing book!

WHILE JUMPING out of an airplane is unusual for a book launch, linking your book's theme to your launch is always a smart idea. The most important thing to remember for a book launch party is to kick back, relax, and enjoy. It is a celebration and a well-deserved nod to the accomplishment that you have achieved. Make sure to savor the moment, and thank all the people who've been there for you. Remember, whether you stay on the ground or not, this is your day. Celebrate it!

YOUR BOOK IS A LIFE-LONG ASSET

You've finished your book! You completed your manuscript and published it. You launched it.

And that's the end of the story. Right?

As we used to say in the eighties, "NOT!"

Writing a book is just the beginning of you sharing of your message. In fact, a book is a content- and event-generating machine!

With a book, you can:

- Land speaking gigs. Why not create a media press kit and share it with event planners, bookstores, and podcast hosts?
- Create social media content. You can use your own book to repurpose content. Share a quote from someone you interviewed from your nonfiction book. Include a steamy quote and an intriguing (hot body!) picture from your rom-com book as an Instagram post. Hold your book in a TikTok video and talk about it.
- Connect with potential clients. If you're a speaker, coach, or consultant, consider giving a copy of your printed book

to a potential, interested client. Use your ebook as a lead magnet to ask people to opt into your email list.

- Raise awareness and funds for nonprofits. If your book is centered on awareness of an issue, consider hosting an event with a nonprofit and including your book for sale or as a giveaway. You'll both benefit as you'll create support for the nonprofit while promoting your book.
- Create valuable relationships. You can reach out and start a book club with interested readers and authors in a similar genre. You can attend book fairs and meet potential readers. Share your knowledge by being a part of a book panel.
- Impact other people's lives. Your message can continue to resonate when you offer to do talks or readings from your book.
- Open doors to new opportunities. You can share your expertise with other authors and lead to additional book publications.
- Leave a legacy for your family. Create a lasting memory for your loved ones by sharing your book with them. Memoirs are a powerful way to speak to generations you may never meet, but they will have the opportunity to get to know you.

Your book is a life-long asset. Years after you have left this earth, others will continue gaining insights from your words. That's incredibly powerful!

"Society grows great when old men plant trees whose shade they will never see."
— James Kerr, Legacy: What the All Blacks Can Teach Us About the Business of Life

---

WHAT NEXT?

The time is now. You have the power to craft your manuscript and share your amazing message, your "business card on steroids," with the world. You've been given something important to share. Who are you to keep it from your readers who want and need it?

If you are writing a book and need help, please contact me and the KWE Publishing team! Our team would love to help you with creating your book. If you'd like to talk about your idea or want advice, we are here for you. Even if we don't work together, I'm happy to share what I know.

Ready for more info, plus a super fun and interesting conversation? Book a 30-minute complimentary consultation by clicking here:

https://kwepubscheduling.as.me/

OUR KWE PUBLISHING team looks forward to hearing about your incredible book project. WRITE ON!

ABOUT THE AUTHOR

Specializing in personal development books and thoughtful children's books is the mission of Kim Wells Eley's company, KWE Publishing. "The common thread of both is to help people see what's possible and shift to a more enjoyable, fulfilled life," she says. As a writing coach and publishing consultant, Kim gives clients six steps to make their books a reality.

Kim is happily married to her BFF and has been for over twenty years. She's a speaker; an author; a resident of Prince George, Virginia; a cat lover; a collector of orchids; and she gets all of her news from comedy shows.

Want to write your book, but you don't know where to start? Please contact Kim at:

Kim Wells Eley
KWE Publishing
(804) 536-1972
kwe@kwepub.com
www.kwepub.com

ALSO BY KIM ELEY

Tickers! What Makes People…Tick! And Pursue a Career They Love

Two Weeks in Barcelona, co-authored with Kim Brundage

Two Weeks in Portland, co-authored with Kim Brundage

REFERENCES

What Are You Writing About? "Mise En Place" For Your Writing

Facebook is the trademark of Facebook, Inc.

Meetup is the trademark of Meetup, Inc.

The Special Ingredient for Writing Success

Popular Mechanics monthly magazine is a trademark of HEARST COMMUNICATIONS, INC.

People magazine is a trademark of Dotdash Meredith.

What to Expect When You're Publishing a Book

Eat Pray Love: One Woman's Search for Everything Across Italy, India and Indonesia by Elizabeth Gilbert. Riverhead Books (February 16, 2006).

Bowker is a trademark of R.R. BOWKER LLC.

Write It Shitty! The First Draft Belongs to the Universe

Anne Lamott, *Bird by Bird: Some Instructions on Writing and Life*. Pantheon Books; 1st edition (May 5, 1994).

Play-Doh is a trademark of HASBRO, INC.

If You Don't Know Where You're Going, You Won't Get There

WAG Your Work: Writing Accountability Groups: Bootcamp for Increasing Scholarly Productivity by Kimberly A. Skarupski, Ph.D., MPH. CreateSpace Independent Publishing Platform (April 1, 2018).

The Life-Changing Magic of Tidying Up: The Japanese Art of Decluttering and Organizing by Marie Kondo. Ten Speed Press; 1st edition (October 14, 2014).

Stop! Ending Your Book is Hard to Do

The Great Gatsby by F. Scott Fitzgerald. Baker Street Press (May 31, 2018).

Book genre info from https://www.writersdigest.com/whats-new/word-count-for-novels-and-childrens-books-the-definitive-post, https://thewritelife.com/how-many-words-in-a-novel/

Launching Your Amazing Book! Celebrate Your Success

Your Secret Superpower: Tame Fear to Thrive by Brian Muka. KWE Publishing, October 2019.

Sharpie pens are a trademark of Sanford, L.P.

Square credit card readers are a trademark of Square, Inc.

Your Book is a Life-Long Asset

Kerr, James. <u>Legacy: What the All Blacks Can Teach Us About the Business of Life.</u> Constable & Robinson (December 17, 2013).

www.ingramcontent.com/pod-product-compliance
Lightning Source LLC
Chambersburg PA
CBHW070033030426

42335CB00017B/2412